Department of the Environment
Ancient Monuments and Historic Buildings

Aldborough Roman Town and Museum

DOROTHY CHARLESWORTH

D1794749

LONDON: HER MAJESTY'S STATIONERY OFFICE

Contents

© *Crown copyright 1970*

First published 1970

Third impression 1976

ISBN 0 11 670175 7

Isurium Brigantum the Roman town at Aldborough

The preservation of the south-west corner of the town wall and of most of the pieces in the museum collection is the result of the interest of the Lawson, later Lawson-Tancred, family over a period of more than a hundred years. Some buildings in the Manor House garden were dug and recorded in H. E. Smith's *Reliquiae Insurianae* published in 1852. These were filled in after excavation but the wall and the quarry outside the south-west angle of the town remained on view and many of the finds were shown in the museum. These were given to the Ministry of Public Building and Works in 1952 by the Dowager Lady Lawson-Tancred, DBE, and a new museum subsequently built.

The name

The town is recorded in Ptolemy's *Geography* as Isurium and in the *Antonine Itinerary* on Routes I and II as Isurium and Route V as Isu. brigantum, Isurium of the Brigantes, the tribe who occupied most of Yorkshire, Lancashire and the counties northwards as far as, if not beyond, the line of Hadrian's Wall in the early first century AD. The name Isurium may be derived from the Celtic name of the River Ure, Isura, but this is not certain.

The town plan

Isurium followed the conventional plan of a small Roman town, a regular grid of streets with the public open space, the forum, near its centre. This is reflected in the plan of the village of Aldborough which lies in the southern two-thirds of the Roman town. The defences enclosed an almost rectangular area of some 55 acres. Four gates gave access. Of these only the position of the north gate has been exactly established, by excavation in 1924 and 1938. The modern road entering the village from the south lies opposite it and the Roman south gate is probably under the road. The west gate must lie under or near the modern road from Boroughbridge where it passes the Manor House. One of the massive stones, said to weigh a ton and half, with the pivot hole in it was found near the Manor House but no other evidence of the gateway is recorded. The east gate stood near Aldborough Hall and indeed until the mid-eighteenth century the road to Lower Dunsforth ran north of its present course, probably on the line of the Roman road. Here again the only structural evidence for the gateway is the discovery of two large stones with pivot holes in them near the Hall.

A by-pass was provided for the traffic between York and the North round the east side of Isurium.

On the south side of the road, between the east and west gates, a range of rooms was found in 1770, extending at least 220ft in length. This is probably the north side of the forum, the rooms being shops and offices, and the open space of the market occupying the present position of the church and churchyard. Its size cannot be calculated nor the position of the public buildings associated with it established. The nearest known feature is a mosaic pavement of unrecorded design, but said by Eckroyd Smith to be the finest of the then existing floors, under the present vicarage. This might be the floor, or part of the floor, of the basilica.

Another feature of the centre of the town was Borough Hill, where several mosaic floors, the foundations of a considerable building, two bases of pillars and box flue-tiles together with small metal objects were found. These are known only from Drake's scanty record of the excavation and the plates in his *Eboracum*, published in 1736. The presence of flue-tiles and presumably also a hypocaust, makes it unlikely that the building was, as he suggested, a temple. It is more likely to have been a private house or a bath-house. The pavements near the Manor House indicate another substantial building, probably a courtyard house.

Most work has been done in the south-west quarter of the town, but no complete building has been excavated under modern conditions. What is recorded as a bath-house was exposed in the Manor House gardens and another building to the south of it was largely dug. Part of the house, containing the two mosaic pavements (pp 6 and 7) now on view, was cleared. A third mosaic from either the same or a neighbouring house was also partly cleared.

The mosaic pavements

The town was rich in pavements. Some found and recorded before 1736 had already vanished by 1852.

The two pavements open to the public are both in their original position and both belong to the same building, partly excavated in the 1840s. This was a large town house, probably built round a courtyard with these two rooms at the north-west end. The first, found in 1832

as a result of an innkeeper digging a hole to bury a calf, is incomplete. A series of borders of conventional patterns surround the central square in which is an animal sitting under a stylised tree. It has been described as a panther or as a lion and is probably a lion. Part of the mane can just be seen. The second, found in 1848, about 4ft below ground, that is 1 to 2ft deeper than the first pavement, is in perfect condition. The central eight-point star is surrounded by four decorative borders, alternating black and white, and red, yellow, white and black to give effective emphasis to the formality of the pavement.

A third pavement, in poor condition, was found to the south-west of these in 1846. It may be from the dining-room of the same house as the two previous pavements. It is certainly not the floor of the basilica, as has been suggested. The room, as shown by H. E. Smith,

is divided into three sections; an ante-chamber at the south-east end
has a broad plain border and a patterned 'door-mat', in the centre;
the main part of the room has two plain borders, a black and white
Greek key, a red, yellow, white and black guilloche, a black and white
Vitruvian scroll and only the extreme corner of the central design with
a mask or face. The apsidal inner end of the room has the remains of
a panelled pattern with two figures, intended to be viewed from the
apse, not the entrance. In one panel HELICON is written in Greek

6

letters, making it plain that the scene depicted was Mount Helicon, the seat of the Muses, and the complete pavement will have shown all nine. This is unique in Britain. On the broad band of plain tesserae round the apse the diners' couches will have stood.

In the Leeds City Museum is a fourth Aldborough pavement, or rather one panel 4ft square from a larger pavement. It was found in the early nineteenth century near the site of the east gate but south of the existing road. This scene also is unique among the known Romano-British pavements. It is a crude representation of the legend of the founders of Rome, Romulus and Remus, being suckled by the wolf. The stylised tree is similar to that on the lion pavement and the crude drawing recalls the Venus pavement found in the villa at Rudston in the East Riding.

A pavement of unrecorded design was under the present vicarage. The mosaics from the house on Borough Hill, recorded by Drake (1736), had vanished by 1852, as had one from the north side of the village street. Another group of mosaics, some parts of a corridor, are recorded near the Manor House. In Aldborough is the greatest concentration of mosaics in the north, where they are otherwise very scarce, and perhaps a permanent school of mosaicists existed here in the fourth century.

The defences

More is known of the defences than of the interior of Isurium. The first defences consisted of an earth bank with a ditch in front of it, constructed in the second half of the second century AD. This was recognised in excavations on the east side of the town in 1965. The first stone gates may have been contemporary with this although timber gate-towers are more often associated with earth ramparts. The excavations at the north gate showed that it had not been erected before the middle of the second century, but apparently not long after that date and this seems to coincide with the construction of the first rampart. The remodelling of the gate, the date being indicated by the discovery of a *denarius* of Severus Alexander (222–235), on the contemporary road surface, should be connected with the alteration to the defences, the insertion of a stone wall in the front of the bank and the renewal of the bank itself. The presence of a worn coin, most probably of Julia Domna, wife of Septimius Severus (193–211), in the wall footings, found in the 1938 excavations, suggests that the wall and re-modelling of the gate were contemporaneous, in about the middle of the third century.

In the final phase bastions were added to the wall, overlying the original ditch, and a new ditch was dug further out from the wall This was done in the mid-fourth century. The bastions will have been regularly spaced round the defences. Their existence has been proved at three angles of the town wall, all except the south-west. On the south side two bastions have been located, each halfway between the south gate and the appropriate corner of the wall. In 1935 the first bastion south of the north-east corner and in 1965 the first bastion south of the east gate were found. The foundations only remained in every case and, except in the case of the bastion east of the south gate dug in 1964, it has been suggested that the shape was more or less semi-circular. The bastion found in 1964 was definitely rectangular.

Visible remains of the defences

The entrance to the site is situated near the south gate of the town and the path leads to the south-west corner of its defences. This area was excavated early in the nineteenth century and preserved as a feature of the Manor House grounds. Its condition in 1852 is described and illustrated by H. Eckroyd Smith.

This stretch of wall illustrates all the features of the town defences, except the bank against the inner face of the wall which was removed by the early excavators. The wall itself is 8ft 6in wide, built of local red sandstone on a foundation of clay and cobble. It has been heavily robbed in the distant past for building stone and now stands only a few courses high. At the back of the wall are two square towers contemporary with the wall and spaced at regular intervals between the gate and the angle. These were probably accessible only from the rampart walk along the top of the wall and used for storing military equipment. A third internal tower can be seen at the corner of the town wall. To the outer face of the wall bastions were added in the mid-fourth century and one is recorded in this sector; nothing but its rubble foundation was seen when the area was re-dug in 1967 and this could not be left exposed. Eckroyd Smith (1852) described it as a 'semi-circular chamber or tower, which occupies 34ft square in the rampart and is secured within by a wall of grey stone 4ft thick, in front of which the foundations project in the centre 25ft'. It projects also behind the wall where its clay and cobble foundation was uncovered in 1967.

A bastion might be expected at the south-west corner, although Eckroyd Smith made no mention of it. A limited area examined in 1973 did not reveal any signs of one. The ground fell away steeply on the outer side of the clay and cobble foundation which was all that remained of the town wall and outer wall of the tower.

Just outside the town (and outside the DOE's guardianship area) is the quarry from which much of the building stone may have come.

The history of the town

The history of the defences, outlined above, is reasonably well established by modern excavation. However, they were laid out round an already existing town and very little is known about it.

There is no suggestion that Isurium was occupied before the Roman period. The few examples of Celtic work in the museum need not be earlier than the Roman occupation. It was not the practice of the Brigantes to live in towns. Their principal settlements were hill-forts, defensible sites such as Almondbury, near Huddersfield, the stronghold of Cartimandua, the last queen of Brigantia, and Stanwix, in the North Riding, where her consort Venutius gathered his forces at the time of the civil war which gave the Roman governor of southern Britain, Petilius Cerialis, an excuse to invade in AD 71 and conquer the tribe which had formerly been Rome's ally.

Many towns in Britain which became an administrative centre of a tribal area, as was Isurium for the Brigantes, started as a settlement outside a Roman fort. At Aldborough no structural remains of a fort have been found, although the site seems to demand one both to fit the plan of forts at regular intervals and to control the river crossing. It has been suggested that the fort was sited on the now vanished Borough Hill, but the area, if early plans are at all accurate, was hardly large enough. A tile of the Ninth Legion might imply military building, but it is an isolated find, and the sudden increase in the number of known coins, 26 of Vespasian (69–79) contrasting with 20 earlier coins ranging from Republican times to the reign of Vitellius, suggests an occupation at the time of, and immediately after, Cerialis' campaigns, but there is little pottery as early as this and pieces of military equipment (which in any case cannot be accurately dated) are so few as to suggest visiting soldiers rather than a garrison. The most important item is the remains of a military badge on show in the museum.

The earliest structural remains are the sleeper-trenches of two Flavian buildings, one outside the north-west corner of the defences, dug in 1935, and another near the north gate, in 1938. A post-hole and first-century pottery was found in a sand-pit behind the wall near the north-west corner. Under a building of Antonine date on the east side of the town post-holes of a timber building were found in 1961. First-century pottery was found near the centre of the town in a pipe-line trench in 1935. These meagre and scattered finds are enough to show that the town grew up in the later years of the first century.

An internal tower and part of the town wall near the south-west corner of the town

The absence of any inscription makes it impossible to determine the time at which Isurium attained its full status as a *civitas*, the recognised economic and political centre of the tribe. In Ptolemy's *Geography* the town appears as merely Isurium but by the time of the *Antonine Itineraries* it is Isurium Brigantum. This gives a wide margin as the *Itineraries* may not represent a date earlier than the third century. There is no evidence either of the date of the public buildings and formal planning of the town but the reign of Hadrian (117–138), when the Roman occupation of the north of Britain was firmly consolidated, seems the most likely time. Most of the known buildings are of third and fourth century date, and, judged by the mosaic pavements and the painted wall plaster found in the nineteenth century excavations, the town was wealthy and flourishing in that period although the lands of the tribe had been reduced. The building of the town wall (see page 8), and three milestones indicating repairs to the roads near the town in the reign of Decius (249–251), demonstrate the community's activity in the mid-third century. The bastions were built a century later and the unrest of the second half of the fourth century must have had its effect on the prosperity of the town. The coins fall off sharply in the reign of Valentinian II (AD 375–392) but repairs to the north gate were made about this time and there are seven coins of Arcadius (395–408) and one of Honorius (395–423) to prove occupation until the very end of the fourth century. Presumably the breakdown of the civil administration was followed by the rapid decay and desertion of the town. The end is as obscure as the beginning. A small collection of Anglian, seventh century, objects probably from a woman's grave and two carved bones of the Viking period in the museum are the only relics of the following five centuries.

The museum

Most of the items in the museum were found in the Manor House garden and were in the museum of the Lawson, later Lawson-Tancred, family who handed it over to the then Ministry of Works in 1952. Other material has been added from excavations in the village.

Everything shown here was found in or near Aldborough and, with few exceptions, is associated with the Roman occupation. Replicas of two important pieces, the terret in the form of the bust of a horned god (original in the Yorkshire Philosophical Society Museum, York) and of a lamp in the form of a sleeping slave-boy (original in the British Museum), are included by courtesy of the two museums.

Metalwork

This is a particularly fine collection of bronze objects from a single site. The bulk of the material is of Roman date, although much of it, being made locally, shows the strong influence of Celtic art. Some later metalwork both of the Anglian and medieval periods is in a small centre case.

The earliest pieces are the terret and three other bronzes, all probably horse trappings, all typically Celtic in design. The terret, the ring through which the reins passed, at the centre of the yoke, is in the form of a bull-horned god, a representation frequently found in stone among the Celts and in various parts of the Brigantian territory. This will have been the property of one of the wealthy war-like Brigantian aristocracy at, or before, the time of the Roman conquest of Brigantia. Originally the shoulders, and probably the eyes, were decorated with enamel and the fearsome head would have faced forwards, towards the enemy. The other pieces, the double loop and the bar decorated with a pelta design, were both mounted on leather. Both are first century AD but not necessarily earlier than the Roman invasion c. AD 71. The pendant with the open-work triskele on the base, which was found in 1938 in excavations of the north wall of Isurium, could be a decorative feature of the harness, like a modern horse brass.

The personal ornaments are slightly later in date and include a number of trumpet and head-stud brooches made in the north of England in the second century. The trumpet brooches with the classical acanthus moulding at the centre of the bow and a Celtic curvilinear design in coloured enamel on the heads of some examples, illustrate the fusion of the two cultures. The brooches were worn in

pairs and on several the loop at the top, through which the linking chain passed, survives. Rings, earrings, decorated hair-pins and dress fasteners are also shown. The finger rings include some key rings, a faceted ring in tinned bronze and gem stones from rings (see page 18). The rectangular dress fastener is a typical north-British example, such as is found outside, as well as within, the Roman province. Most of these personal ornaments are in the first case on the right as you look down the museum. Bronze strap-ends and various decorative pieces which would originally be fixed to leather are in the neighbouring case.

A number of bronze and iron objects of domestic use are shown in the other desk cases. These include keys and the remains of locks, parts of door latches, T-shaped holdfasts, a number of bronze studs which would have been fixed to leather, and bronze angle-pieces from a wooden box. The bronze handle and part of the side fixing is preserved from a small bucket of wood or leather which has totally decayed. The complete decay of part of the object and the survival of only the metal, frequently in poor condition, often makes interpretation of the fragments impossible. One example of this is the small fore-part of a boar made to attach on to something unknown. The bronze

lion's paw, however, is clearly the remains of the foot of a table or chair and is a reminder that the furniture of the larger houses will have been of a standard in keeping with the mosaic floors and painted walls. Of the knives, the blades only in most cases survived but there is also one unusual handle of iron with bronze strips inlaid. It is shown with *styli*, similarly decorated, which have a sharp end for writing on wax tablets and a flat end for erasing. Toilet articles, mainly in bronze, include a back scratcher in the form of a hand, ear-picks, nail-cleaners and spatulae.

Some pieces of military equipment have been found on the site and present the problem of whether or not there was a fort here before the town (see page 10). There are iron javelin, arrow and spear-heads and part of an openwork bronze badge with an incomplete inscription.

A lead vessel used to hold a cremation stands in the centre case, with the pottery.

Coins

A few of the less worn and better preserved coins are shown. The obverse with the portrait of the Emperor is generally displayed, but an example of the Britannia reverse, which may be compared with that on the modern 50p, is shown. The earliest coin is not a Roman one but one used by the tribe of the Dobunni. It is not known how it reached Aldborough. The entire collection consists of over 1000 coins, mainly bronze, covering the whole period of the Roman occupation of Isurium.

Pottery

The complete vessels are all displayed in the cases at the end of the museum but some fragments are shown in the desk cases. The pottery can be divided into wares made in Britain and those imported.

The bulk of the pottery was made in Britain and includes some fine examples of coloured-coated wares made in the Nene valley from the late second century onwards, the most striking of which is the incomplete hunt cup from the 1961 excavations. Most of the pottery, however, is 'kitchen-ware', pie-dishes, cooking pots, mixing bowls (mortaria) some with the maker's name stamped on the rim, but a few fragmentary examples of finer wares which may have been made in Brigantia have been found. These include pieces with stamped decoration (some stamped pottery was found in kilns at Cantley, Doncaster) and pieces with red painted stripes in shapes copied from the samian ware of Gaul.

The right-hand case holds the complete vessels and a selection of the large quantity of fragments of samian ware found in Aldborough. This red tableware comes mainly from Central Gaul. It was imported from the earliest years of the Roman occupation until the beginning of the third century AD. Examples on display illustrate the most common shapes and styles of decoration, the bowls with figures in relief which were made in a mould, the rouletting, cutting and barbotine decoration on the wheel-turned dishes. There are several examples of potter's stamps, on the centre of the plain dishes and among the decoration on the moulded bowls. The black samian is a less common find.

Other imported pottery is from the Cologne and Trier area, a drinking vessel and bowl with dark, metallic-looking surfaces, and wine jars (amphorae) which were imported for their contents and not for themselves. No complete example has survived, but a substantial part of the base of a narrow, carrot-shaped amphora is shown and handles from others.

Two pieces of green glazed medieval pottery can be seen in the centre case.

Tiles

Tiles were used for roofs, floors and the flues of central-heating systems of private and public bath houses or other heated rooms in a private residence. There is no complete example and those on display are part of a roof tile (*tegula*) with a flanged edge and an animal footprint on it and two flue tiles with incised patterns to which the wall plaster could be keyed. The thinner tile with the more complicated pattern is part of a box tile, which formed a flue for the heat to be carried up in the thickness of the wall.

Glass

Most of the glass is from ordinary square and cylindrical bottles of first and second century date. The tops survive better than the thinner bodies. One example of a marked base is shown. There are a few pieces of finer vessels, the base of a drinking glass or small flask with snake-thread decoration and the rim of a fourth-century beaker with dark blue dots on it. There is one glass gaming counter made from a thick piece of bottle. Pottery fragments and flat stones were also shaped into counters.

Bone

Pins, needles and spoons are quite common and some are decorated. There are also gaming counters and two dice, which are exactly the same as the modern dice. Fragments of two fine-toothed combs are shown with the other toilet implements. Two decorated bone ornaments of ninth–tenth century date are isolated finds of the Viking occupation of the area round York.

Gemstones

There are only two of these, although it was quite common Roman practice to wear a seal-ring. The more elaborate is a jasper intaglio depicting a hare in a chariot pulled by a cock. The blue agate intaglio shows a standing nude figure with his right hand outstretched.

Stone

Four inscribed stones, the earliest found in 1776, and one piece of sculpture are in the museum and there are other examples, an uninscribed altar, a capital and quernstones in the grounds.

Two of the inscriptions are on milestones, circular or oval in section and when complete standing about 4ft high. Both were set up in the reign of Decius (AD 249–251) and must indicate repairs to the roads at that time. Nothing is recorded about the discovery of the top of an altar to Jupiter and the Mother Goddesses and the tombstone of Felicula, found in 1811. The damaged figure of Mercury with his staff by his right foot looks as though it has been re-used as a building stone at some time. Another figure of Mercury can be seen in the church.

Glossary

ACANTHUS	Prickly-leaved plant; design based on its leaf.
AMPHORA	Two-handled vessel.
APSIDAL	Of the form of an apse.
APSE	Semi-circular end to, or projection from, a building.
BASILICA	Royal palace; oblong hall with double colonnade and apse.
BASTION	Projection from the general outline of a fortress from which the garrison can see, and defend by flanking fire, the ground before the ramparts.
GUILLOCHE	Architectural ornament imitating braded ribbons.
INTAGLIO	Engraved design; carving in hard material; gem with incised design.
MOSAIC	Picture produced by joining minute pieces of glass, stone, etc., of different colours.
RAMPART	Mass of excavated earth on which the troops and guns of the garrison are elevated.
TERRET	Each of loops or rings on harness-pad for driving reins to pass through.
SAMIAN	Fine pottery found on Roman sites.

CONVERSION TABLE

Page 3	55 acres	22 hectares
4	220ft	6.7m
5	4ft	1.2m
6	10ft 6in	3.15m
7	12ft	3.7m
9	8ft 6in	2.6m
	34ft	10.0m
	25ft	7.6m

Printed in Scotland by Her Majesty's Stationery Office at HMSO Press, Edinburgh
Dd 496917 K50 10/76 (13719)